FAVOURITE
FLOWER POEMS

This edition first published in the United Kingdom in 2016 by

National Trust Books
1 Gower Street
London WC1E 6HD

An imprint of Pavilion Books Company Ltd

First published as *Ode to Flowers* in 2013 by Batsford.

ISBN: 9781909881747

A CIP catalogue record for this book is available from the British Library.

20 19 18 17 16
10 9 8 7 6 5 4 3 2

Repro by Mission Productions Ltd, Hong Kong
Printed by GPS group, Slovenia

This book can be ordered direct from the publisher at the website:
www.pavilionbooks.com, or try your local bookshop. Also available at
National Trust shops and www.nationaltrustbooks.co.uk

FAVOURITE
FLOWER POEMS

CARE

There are mistakes of
spelling and grammar in
this book
Excerpts from poems are
not marked as such

National Trust

Contents

To a Snowdrop

Lone Flower, hemmed in with snows, and white as they,
But hardier far, once more I see thee bend
They forehead as if fearful to offend,
Like an unbidden guest. Though day by day
Storms, sallying from the mountain-tops, waylay
The rising sun, and on the plains descend;
Yet art thou welcome, welcome as a friend
Whose Zeal outruns his promise! Blue-eyed May
Shall soon behold this border thickly set
With bright jonquils, their odours lavishing
On the soft west-wind and his frolic peers;
Nor will I then thy modest grace forget,
Chaste Snowdrop, venturous harbinger of Spring,
And pensive monitor of fleeting years!

William Wordsworth
(1770–1850)

A Contemplation upon Flowers

Brave flowers–that I could gallant it like you,
  And be as little vain!
You come abroad, and make a harmless show,
  And to your beds of earth again.
You are not proud: you think your birth:
For your embroider'd garments are from earth.

You do obey your months and times, but I
  Would have it ever Spring:
My fate would know no Winter, never die,
  Nor think of such a thing.
O that I could my bed of earth but view
And smile, and look as cheerfully as you!

O teach me to see Death and not to fear,
  But rather to take truce!
How often have I seen you at a bier,
  And there look fresh and spruce!
You fragrant flowers! then teach me, that my breath
Like yours may sweeten and perfume my death.

Henry King
Bishop of Chichester (1592–1669)

Evening Primrose

When once the sun sinks in the west,
And drewdrops pearl the evening's breast;
Almost as pale as moonbeams are,
Or its companionable star,
The evening primrose opes anew
Its delicate blossoms to the dew;
And, hermit-like, shunning the light,
Wastes its fair bloom upon the night;
Who, blindfold to its fond caresses,
Knows not the beauty he possesses.
Thus it blooms on till night is by
And day looks out with open eye,
Abashed at the gaze it cannont shun,
It faints and withers, and is gone.

John Clare
(1793–1864)

The Bluebells (Part)

We stood upon the grass beside the road,
At a wood's fence, to look among the trees.
In windless noon the burning May-time glowed.
Gray, in young green, the beeches stood at ease.
Light speckled in the wood as left it dim:
There lay a blue in which no ship could swim,
Within whose peace no water ever flowed.

Within that pool no shadow ever showed;
Tideless was all that mystery of blue.
Out of eternities man never knew
A living growth man never reaped nor sowed
Snatched in the dim its fitness from the hour
A miracle unspeakable of flower
That tears in the heart's anguish answered-to.

How paint it; how describe? None has the power.
It only had the power upon the soul
To consecrate the spirit and the hour,
To light to sudden rapture and console,
Its beauty called a truce: forgave: forgot
All the long horror of man's earthly lot,
A miracle unspeakable of flower
In a green May unutterably blue.

John Masefield
(1878–1967)

A Church Calendar of English Flowers

The Snowdrop in purest white arraie
First rears her hedde on Candlemass Daie:
While the Crocus hastens to the shrine
Of Primrose love on St Valentine.
Then comes the Daffodil beside
Our Ladye's Smock at our Ladye's tide;
Aboute St George, when blue is worn,
The blue Harebells the field adorn.
Against the daie of the Holy Cross,
The Crowfoot gilds the flowrie grass.
When St Barnabie bright smiles night and daie,
Poor Ragged Robin blooms in the haye.
The scarlet Lychnis, the garden's pride,
Flames of S. John the Baptist's tide;
From Visitation to S. Swithin's showers,
The Lillie white reigns Queen of the Flowers,
And Poppies a sanguine mantle spread,
For the blood of the dragon St Margaret shed.
Then under the wanton Rose agen,
That blushes for penitent Magdalen,
Till Lammas Daie, called August's Wheel,
When the long Corn smells of Cammomile.
When Marie left us here belowe,
The Virgin's Bower is full in blow;
And yet anon the full Sunflower blew,
And became a star for St Bartholomew.
The Passion Flower long has blowed,
To betoken us signs of the holie rood;
The Michaelmas Dasie among dede weeds,
Blooms for St Michael's valorous deeds,

And seems the last of the flowers that stood,
Till the feste of St Simon and St Jude,
Save Mushrooms and the Fungus race
That grow till All Hallowtide takes place.
Soon the evergreen Laurel alone is greene,
When Catherine crowns all learned menne;
Then Ivy and Holly berries are seen,
And Yule Clog and Wassail come round agen.

Anonymous

To Flowers From Italy in Winter

Sunned in the South, and here to-day;
    –If all organic things
Be sentient, flowers, as some men say,
    What are your ponderings?

How can you stay, nor vanish quite
    From this bleak spot of thorn,
And birch, and fir, and frozen white
    Expanse of the forlorn?

Frail luckless exiles hither brought!
    Your dust will not regain
Old sunny haunts of Classic thought
    When you shall waste and wain;

But mix with alien earth, be lit
    With frigid Boreal flame,
And not a sign remain in it
    To tell man whence you came.

Thomas Hardy
(1840–1928)

Daysies

From *Legend of Good Women*

Now have I than swich a condicioun
That, of alle the floures in the mede,
That love I most these floures whyte and rede,
Swiche as men callen daysies in our toun.
To hem have I so greet affedccioun,
As I seyde erst, when comen is the May,
That in my bed ther daweth me no day
That I nam up, and walking in the mede
To seen this floure agein the sonne sprede,
Whan hit up-riseth erly by the morwe;
That blisful sighte softneth al my sorwe,
So glad am I whan that I have presence
Of hit, to doon al maner reverence,
As She, that is of alle floures flour,
Fulfilled of al vertu and honour,
And ever y-lyke fair, and fresh of hewe;
And I love hit, and ever y-lyke newe,
And ever shal, til that myn herte dye;
Al swete I nat, of this I wol nat lye,
Ther loved no wight hotter in his lyve.

Geoffrey Chaucer
(c. 1340–1400)

Hillside Flowers

From *Thyrsis*

I know these slopes; who knows them if not I?–
But many a dingle on the loved hillside,
With thorns once studded, old, white-blossom'd trees,
Where thick the cowslips grew, and far descried
High tower'd the spikes of purple orchises,
Hath since our day put by
The coronals of that forgotten time;
Down each green bank hath gone the ploughboy's team,
And only in the hidden brookside gleam
Primroses, orphans of the flowery prime.

Matthew Arnold
(1822–88)

The Marigold

When with a serious musing I behold
The grateful and obsequious marigold,
How duly every morning she displays
Her open breast, when Titan spreads his rays;
How she observes him in his daily walk,
Still bending towards him her small tender stalk;
How, when he down declines, she droops and mourns,
Bedewed, as 'twere with tears, till he returns;
And how she veils her flowers when he is gone,
As if she scorned to be looked on
By an inferior eye; or did contemn
To wait upon a meaner light than him.
When this I meditate, methinks the flowers
Have spirits far more generous than ours,
And give us fair examples to despise
The servile fawnings and idolatries,
Wherewith we court these earthly things below,
Which merit not the service we bestow.

George Wither
(1588–1667)

The Woodspurge

The wind flapped loose, the wind was still,
Shaken out dead from tree and hill:
I had walked on at the wind's will,—
I sat now, for the wind was still.

Between my knees my forehead was,—
My lips, drawn in, said not Alas!
My hair was over in the grass,
My naked ears heard the day pass.

My eyes, wide open, had the run
Of some ten weeds to fix upon;
Among those few, out of the sun,
The woodspurge flowered, three cups in one.

From perfect grief there need not be
Wisdom or even memory;
One thing then learnt remains to me,—
The woodspurge has a cup of three.

D. G. Rossetti
(1828–1882)

Wild Flowers

From *A Midsummer Night's Dream*

I know a banke where the wilde time blowes,
Where Oxslips and the nodding Violet growes,
Quite over-cannoped with luscious woodbine,
With sweet muske roses, and with Eglantine:
There sleepes Tytania, sometime of the night,
Lul'd in these flowers, with dances and delight:
And there the snake throwes her enamel'd skinne,
Weed wide enough to wrappe a Fairy in.
And with the juyce of this Ile streake her eyes,
And make her full of hateful fantasies.

William Shakespeare
(1564–1616)

The Lily of the Valley

Some flowers there are that rear their heads on high,
The gorgeous products of a burning sky,
That rush upon the eye with garish bloom,
And make the senses drunk with high perfume.
Not such art thou, sweet Lily of the Vale!
So lovely, small, and delicately pale,–
We might believe, if such fond faith were ours,
As sees humanity in trees and flowers,
That thou wert once a maiden, meek and good,
That pined away beneath her native wood
For very fear of her own loveliness,
And died of love she never would confess.

Hartley Coleridge
(1796–1849)

The Rose

O Rose, thou flower of flowers, thou fragrant wonder,
  Who shall describe thee in thy ruddy prime,
  Thy perfect fullness in the summertime,
When the pale leaves blushingly part asunder
And show the warm red heart lies glowing under?
  Thou shouldst bloom surely in some sunny clime,
  Untouched by blights and chilly winter's rime,
Where lightnings never flash nor peals the thunder.
And yet in happier spheres they cannot need thee
  So much as we do with our weight of woe;
Perhaps they would not tend, perhaps not heed thee,
  And thou wouldst lonely and neglected grow;
And He who is all wise, He hath decreed thee
  To gladden earth and cheer all hearts below.

Christina Rossetti
(1830–1894)

Flowers

What favourite flowers are mind, I cannot say–
My fancy changes with the summer's day.
Sometimes I think, agreeing with the Bees,
That my best flowers are those tall apple trees,
Who give a Bee his cyder while in bloom,
And keep me waiting till their apples come.
Sometimes I think the Columbine has won,
Who hangs her head and never looks the Sun
Straight in the face. And now the Golden Rod
Beckons me over with a graceful nod;
Shaped like a sheaf of corn, her ruddy skin
Drinks the Sun dry, and leaves his splendor thin.
Sometimes I think the Rose must have her place–
And then the Lily shakes her golden dice
Deep in a silver cup, to win or lose.
So I go on, from Columbine to Rose,
From Marigold to Flock, from Flock to Thrift–
Till nothing but my garden stones are left.
But when I see the dimples in her face,
All filled with tender moss in every place–
Ah, then I think, when all is said and done,
My favourite flower must be the Mossy Stone!

W. H. Davies
(1871–1940)

Jasmine

From *Lalla Rookh*

Twas midnight–through the lattice, wreath'd
With woodbine, many a perfume breath'd
From plants that wake when others sleep,
From timid jasmine buds, that keep
Their odour to themselves all day,
But, when the sun-light dies away,
Let the delicious secret out
To every breeze that roams about.

Thomas Moore
(1779–1852)

The Odours
of Flowers

From *Milton, The Book of Second*

Thou percievest the Flowers put forth their precious Odours,
And none can tell how from so small a center comes such sweets.
Forgetting that within that Center Eternity expends
Its ever during doors that Og & Anak fiercely guard.
First, e'er the morning breaks, joy opens in the flowery bosoms,
Joy even to tears, which the Sun rising dries; first the Wild Thyme
And Meadow-sweet, downy & soft waving among the reeds,
Light springing on the air, lead the sweet Dance: they wake
The Honeysuckle sleeping on the Oak; the flaunting beauty
Revels along upon the wind; the White-thorn, lovely May,
Opens her many lovely eyes; listening, the Rose still sleeps,
None dare to wake her; soon she bursts her crimson curtain'd bed
And comes forth in the majesty of beauty; every Flower,
The Pink, the Jessamine, the Wall-flower, the Carnation,
The Jonquil, the Milk Lilly, opes her heavens; every Tree
And Flower & Herb soon fill the air with an innumerable Dance,
Yet all in order sweet & lovely.

William Blake
(1757–1827)

A Garden

Written after the Civil War

See how the flowers, as at parade,
Under their colours stand display'd:
Each regiment in order grows,
That of the tulip, pink, and rose.
But when the vigilant patrol
Of stars walks round about the pole,
Their leaves, that to the stalks are curl'd,
Seem to their staves the ensigns furl'd.
Then in some flower's beloved hut
Each bee, as sentinel, is shut,
And sleeps so too; but if once stirr'd,
She runs you through, nor asks the word.
    O thou, that dear and happy Isle,
The garden of the world erewhile,
Thou Paradise of the four seas
Which Heaven planted us to please,
But, to exclude the world, did guard
With wat'ry, if not flaming, sword;
What luckless apple did we taste
To make us mortal and thee waste!
Unhappy! Shall we never more
That sweet militia restore,
When gardens only had their towers,
And all the garrisons were flowers;
When roses only arms might bear,
And men did rosy garlands wear?

Andrew Marvell
(1621–1678)

CELANDINE
BLUE BELL
COWSLIP
WOOD SORREL
SNOWDROP
RAGGED ROBIN
RED
WILD STRAWBERRY
HORSESHOE VETCH
CAMPION
VIOLET
PERIWINKLE
CLOVER
ORCHIS
PRIMROSE
WIND FLOWER
STITCHWORT
HERB ROBERT
PINK TIPPED DAISY
COLT'S-FOOT
DAFFODIL
LADY'S SMOCK
OX-EYE DAISY
LORDS & LADIES
BEAKED PARSLEY
YARROW
BUTTERCUP
SPEEDWELL
CHARLOCK
GROUND IVY
KING-CUP

SPRING

To The Aconite

Flower, that foretell'st a Spring thou ne'er shalt see,
Yet smilest still upon thy wintry day,
Content with thy joy-giving destiny,
Nor envying fairer flowers their festal May,–
O golden-chaliced Aconite! I'll lay
To heart the lesson that thou teachest me;
I, too, contented with my times will be,
And still a placid aspect will display
In tempest-troubled seasons,–nor repine
That others, coming after, shall enjoy
A calmer day, a sunnier sky than mine;
To speed the present, be my sweet employ;–
To cast into a stormy world my mite
Of cheer, like thee, gloom-gliding Aconite!

Thomas Noel
(1799–1861)

Daffodils

I wander'd lonely as a cloud
    That floats on high o'er vales and hills,
When all at once I saw a crowd,
    A host, of golden daffodils;
Beside the lake, beneath the trees,
Fluttering and dancing in the breeze.

Continuous as the stars that shine
    And twinkle on the Milky Way,
They stretch'd in never-ending line
    Along the margin of a bay:
Ten thousand saw I at a glance,
Tossing their heads in sprightly dance.

The waves beside them danced, but they
    Out-did the sparkling waves in glee:
A poet could not but be gay,
    In such a jocund company:
I gazed–and gazed–but little thought
What wealth the show to me had brought.

For oft, when on my couch I lie
    In vacant or in pensive mood,
They flash upon that inward eye
    Which is the bliss of solitude;
And then my heart with pleasure fills,
And dances with the daffodils.

William Wordsworth
(1770–1850)

The Poppies

Like lips behind a veil
The poppies rest under the oats
Lips parting in sleep,
As though night were hot about them,
Touching the souls they speak for with sensual fires;
These lips not petals.

But here it is summer morning,
Cool after the pride-shower;
The smoke goes up in prayer from the village,
And the hills are monks stooping under a hood of mist.
This is surely a virgin moment.

Then what is this fantasy of the poppies?

Richard Church
(1893-1972)

The Primrose

Ask me why I send you here
This sweet Infanta of the year?
Ask me why I send to you
This primrose, thus bepearl'd with dew?
I will whisper to your ears: -
The sweets of love are mix'd with tears.

Ask me why this flower does show
So yellow-green, and sickly too?
Ask me why the stalk is weak
And bending (yet it doth not break)?
I will answer:– These discover
What fainting hopes are in a lover.

Attributed to Robert Herrick (1591–1674) or John Carew (1594–1640)

The Fear of Flowers

The nodding oxeye bends before the wind
The woodbine quakes lest boys their flowers should find,
And prickly dogrose spite of its array
Can't dare the blossom-seeking hand away,
While thistles wear their heavy knobs of bloom
Proud as a warhorse wears its haughty plume,
And by the roadside danger's self defy;
On commons where pined sheep and oxen lie
In ruddy pomp and ever thronging mood
It stands and spreads like danger in a wood,
And in the village street where meanest weeds
Can't stand untouched to fill their husks with seeds,
The haughty thistle o'er all danger towers,
In every place the very wasp of flowers.

John Clare
(1793–1864)

The Love of Flowers

I love flowers too; not for a young girl's reason,
But because these brief visitors to us
Rise yearly from the neighbourhood of the dead,
To show us how far fairer and more lovely
Their world is; and return thither again,
Like parting friends that beckon us to follow,
And lead the way silent and smilingly.
Fair is the season when they come to us,
Unfolding the delights of that existence
Which is below us: 'tis the time of spirits,
Who with the flowers, and, like them, leave their graves:
But when the earth is sealed, and none dare come
Upwards to cheer us, and man's left alone,
We have cold, cutting winter.

Thomas Lovell Beddoes
(1803–1849)

Whinlands

All year round the whin
Can show a blossom or two
But it's in full bloom now.
As if the small yolf stain

From the bird's eggs in
All the nests of the spring
Were spiked and hung
Everywhere on bushes to ripen.

Hills oxidize gold.
Above the smoulder of the green shoot
And dross of dead thorns underfoot
The blossoms scald.

Put a match under
Whins, they go up of a sudden.
They make no flame in the sun
But a fierce heat tremor

Yet incineration like that
Only takes the thorn.
The tough sticks don't burn,
Remain like bone, charred horn.

Gilt, jaggy, springy, frilled
This stunted, dry richness
Persists on hills, near stone ditches,
Over flintbed and battlefield.

Seamus Heaney
(1939– 2013)

The Snowdrop

Fear thou no more, thou timid Flower!
Fear thou no more the winter's might,
The whelming thaw, the ponderous shower,
The silence of the freezing night!
Since Laura murmur'd o'er thy leaves
The potent sorceries of song,
To thee, meek Flowret! gentler gales
   And cloudless skies belong.

...

The petals boast a white more soft,
The spell hath so perfuméd thee,
That careless Love shall deem thee oft
A blossom from his Myrtle tree,
Then laughing at the fair deceit
Shall race with some Etesian wind
To seek the woven arboret
   Where Laura lies reclin'd.

Samuel Taylor Coleridge
(1772–1834)

The Greenhouse

From *The Task*

Who loves a garden loves a green-house too.
Unconscious of a less propitious clime,
There blooms exotic beauty, warm and snug,
While the winds whistle and the snows descend.
The spiry myrtle with unwith'ring leaf
Shines there, and flourishes. The golden boast
Of Portugal and western India there,
The ruddier orange, and the paler lime,
Peep through their polish'd foliage at the storm,
And seem to smile at what they need not fear.
Th' amomum there with intermingling flow'rs
And cherries hangs her twigs. Geranium boasts
Her crimson honours, and the spangled beau,
Ficoides, glitters bright and the winter long.
All plants, of ev'ry leaf, that can endure
The winter's frown, if screen'd from his shrewd bite,
Live there, and prosper. Those Ausonia claims,
Levantine regions these; th' Azores send
Their Jessamine, her Jessamine remote
Caffraia: foreigners from many lands,
They form one social shade, as if conven'd
By magic summons of th' Orphean lyre.
Yet just arrangement, rarely brought to pass
But by a master's hand, disposing well
The gay diversities of leaf and flow'r,
Must lend its aid t' illustrate all their charms,
And dress the regular yet various scene.

William Cowper
(1731–1800)

Cowslips

Our orange wood and lemon glade
No higher than the grass is laid;
You could not walk beneath its bells
Rung heavy with the orchard smells,
But bend down to the cow's soft lip;
And see the honey lamps they sip.

These cowslips in a spring night born
Grow gentle soft and wear no thorn,
Then roll their sweetness to a ball,
The hush of breath, confining all,
Makes orange smell and lemon scent
Into a flowery parliament
Where every cowslip talks, as one,
And nothing, but that scent, is done.

Sacheverell Sitwell
(1897–1988)

The Yellow Violet

When beechen buds begin to swell,
    And woods the blue-bird's warble know,
The yellow violet's modest bell
    Peeps from the last year's leaves below.

Ere russet fields their green resume,
    Sweet flower, I love, in forest bare,
To meet thee, when thy faint perfume
    Alone is in the virgin air.

Of all her train, the hands of Spring
    First plant thee in the watery mould,
And I have seen thee blossoming
    Beside the snow-bank's edges cold.

Thy parent sun, who bade thee view
    Pales skies, and chilling moisture sip,
Has bathed thee in his own bright hue,
And streaked with jet thy glowing lip.

Yet slight thy form, and low thy seat,
    And earthward bent thy gentle eye,
Unapt the passing view to meet,
    When loftier flowers are flaunting nigh.

Oft, in the sunless April day,
    Thy early smile has stayed my walk;
But midst the gorgeous blooms of May,
    I passed thee on thy humble stalk

So they, who climb to wealth, forget
    The friends in darker fortunes tried.
I copied them – but I regret
    That I should ape the ways of pride.

And when again the genial hour
    Awakes the painted tribes of light,
I'll not o'erlook the modest flower
    That made the woods of April bright.

William Cullen Bryant
(1794–1878)

The Blossome

Little think'st thou, poore flower,
    Whom I have watched sixe or seaven dayes,
And seene thy birth, and seene what every houre
Gave to thy growth, thee to this height raise,
And now dost laugh and triumph on this bough,
    Little think'st thou
That it will freeze anon, and that I shall
To morrow find thee falne, or not at all.

Little think'st thou poore heart
That labour'st yet to nestle thee,
And think'st by hovering here to get a part
In a forbidden or forbidding tree,
And hop'st her stiffenesse by long siege to bow:
    Little think'st thou
That thou to morrow, ere that Sunne doth wake,
Must with this Sunne, and mee a journey take.

John Donne
(1573–1631)

To a Friend Who Sent Me Some Roses

As late I rambled in the happy fields,
>What time the skylark shakes the tremulous dew
>From his lush clover covert: –when anew
Adventurous knights take up their dinted shields;
I saw the sweetest flower wild nature yields,
>A fresh-blown musk-rose; 'twas the first that threw
>Its sweets upon the summer; graceful it grew
As is the wand that queen Titania wields.
And, as I feasted on its fragrancy,
>I thought the garden-rose it far excell'd;
But when, O Wells! Thy roses came to me,
>My sense with their deliciousness was spell'd:
Soft voices had they, that with tender plea
>Whisper'd of peace, and truth, and friendliness
unquell'd.

John Keats
(1795–1821)

It Will Be Summer – Eventually

It will be Summer eventually.
Ladies - with parasols -
Sauntering gentlemen - with canes -
And little girls - with dolls -

Will tint the pallid landscape -
As 'twere a bright bouquet -
Though drifted deep, in Parian -
The village lies - today -

The lilacs - bending many a year -
Will sway with purple load -
The bees - will not despise the tune -
Their forefathers - have hummed -

The wild rose - redden in the bog -
The aster - on the hill
Her everlasting fashion - set -
And covenant gentians - frill -

Till summer folds her miracle -
As women - do - their gown -
Or priests - adjust the symbols -
When sacrament - is done -

Emily Dickinson
(1830–1886)

Golden Glories

The buttercup is like a golden cup,
The marigold is like a golden frill,
The daisy with a golden eye looks up,
And golden spreads the flag beside the rill,
And gay and golden nods the daffodil,
The gorsey common swells a golden sea,
The cowslip hangs a head of golden tips,
And golden drops the honey which the bee
Sucks from sweet hearts of flowers, and stores and sips.

Christina Rossetti
(1830–1894)

Lilacs

Lilacs,
False blue,
White,
Purple,
Colour of lilac,
Your great puffs of flowers
Are everywhere in this my New England.
Among your heart-shaped leaves
Orange orioles hop like music-box birds and sing
Their little weak soft songs;
In the crooks of your branches
The bright eyes of song sparrows sitting on spotted eggs
Peer restlessly through the light and shadow
Of all Spring.

Amy Lowell
(1874–1925)

Spring Garland

From *A Winter's Tale, Act IV*

Now, my first Friend
I would I had some Flowers o'th Spring, that might
Become your time of day: and yours, and yours,
That were upon your Virgin-branches yet
Your maiden heads growing; O Proserpina,
For the Flowres now, that (frighted) thou let'st fall
From Dis's Waggon! Daffodils,
That come before the Swallow dares, and take
The windes of March with beauty: Violets dim,
But sweeter than the lids of Juno's eyes,
Or Cytherea's breath; pale Prime-roses,
That die unmarried, ere they can behold
Bright Phœbus in his strength – a Maladie
Most incident to Maids; bold Oxslips, and
The Crowne Imperial: Lillies of all kinds,
The Flowre-de-Luce being one. O, these I lacke,
To make you Garlands of, and my sweet friend,
To strew him o'er and o'er.

William Shakespeare
(1564–1616)

Elegy

Mourn, little harebells o'er the lea;
Ye stately foxgloves fair to see;
Ye woodbines hanging bonnilie,
    In scented bowers;
Ye roses on yon thorny tree,
      The first o' flowers!

At dawn, when every grassy blade
Droops with a diamond at his head,
At ev'n, when beans their fragrance shed
    I' th' rustling gale,
Ye maukins, whiddin; throu' the glade,
      Come, join my wail!

Mourn, Spring, thou darling of the year!
Ilk cowslip cup shall kep a tear;
Thou, Simmer, while each corny spear
    Shoots up his head,
Thy gay, green, flow'ry tresses shear,
      For him that's dead.

Robert Burns
(1759–1796)

Flowers in Winter

From *The Task*, Book 6, *Winter Walk at Noon*

Th' icy touch
Of unprolific winter has impress'd
A cold stagnation on th' intestine tide.
But let the months go round, a few short months,
And all shall be restored. These naked shoots,
Barren as lances, among which the wind
Makes wintry music, sighing as it goes,
Shall put their graceful foliage on again,
And more aspiring, and with ampler spread,
Shall boast new charms, and more than they have lost.
Then each, in its peculiar honours clad,
Shall publish, even to the distant eye,
Its family and tribe. Laburnum, rich
In streaming gold, syringe, iv'ry pure;
The scented and the scentless rose; this red,
And of an humbler growth, the other tall,
And throwing up into the darkest gloom
Of neighb'ring cypress, or more sable yew,
Her silver globes, light as the foamy surf
That the wind severs from the broken wave;
The lilac, various in array, now white,
Now sanguine, and her beauteous head now set
With purple spikes pyramidal, as if
Studious of ornament, yet unresolved
Which hue she most approved, she chose them all;
Copious of flowers the woodbine, pale and wan
But well compensating her sickly looks
With never-cloying odours, early and late;
Hypericum all bloom so thick a swarm
Of flow'rs, like flies clothing her slender rods,

That scarce a leaf appears, mezerion too,
Tough leafless, well attir'd, and thick beset
With blushing wreaths, investing ev'ry spray;
Althæa the purple eye; the broom,
Yellow and bright, as bullion unalloy'd,
Her blossoms; and luxuriant above all
The jasmine, throwing wide her elegant sweets,
The deep dark green of whose unvarnish'd leaf
Makes more conspicuous, and illumines more
The bright profusion of her scatter'd stars. –
These have been, and these shall be in their day;
And all this uniform, uncolour'd scene
Shall be dismantled of its fleecy load
And flush into variety again.

William Cowper
(1731-1800)

To Blossoms

Fair pledges of a fruitful tree,
    Why do ye fall so fast?
    Your date is not so past
But you may stay here yet a while
    To blush and gently smile
        And go at last.

What! Were ye born to be
    An hour or half's delight,
    And so to bid good night?
'Twas pity Nature brought you forth
    Merely to show your worth
        And lose you quite.

But you are lovely leaves, where we
    May read how soon things have
    Their end, though n'er so brave:
And after they have shown their pride
    Like you a while, they glide
        Into the grave.

Robert Herrick
(1591-1674)

The Snowdrop

Now – now, as low I stooped, thought I,
I will see what this snowdrop is;
So shall I put much argument by,
    And solve a lifetime's mysteries.

A northern wind had frozen the grass;
Its blades were hoar with crystal rime,
Aglint like light-dissecting glass
    At beam of morning-prime.

From hidden bulb the flower reared up
Its angled, slender, cold, dark stem,
Whence dangled an inverted cup
    For tri-leaved diadem.

Beneath these ice-pure sepals lay
A triplet of green pencilled snow,
Which in the chill-aired gloom of day
    Stirred softly to and fro.

Mind fixed, but else made vacant, I,
Lost to my body, called my soul
To don that frail solemnity,

Its inmost self my goal.
And though in vain – no mortal mind
Across that threshold yet hath fared! –
In this collusion I divined
  Some consciousness we shared.

Strange roads –while suns, a myriad, set –
Has led us through infinity;
And where they crossed, there then had met
  Not two of us but three.

Walter de la Mare
(1873–1956)

The First Dandelion

Simple and fresh and fair from winter's close emerging,
As if no artifice of fashion, business, politics had ever been
Forth from its sunny nook of sheltered grass – innocent,
　　Golden, calm as the dawn,
The spring's first dandelion shows it's trustful face.

Walt Whitman
(1819–1892)

Spring Flowers

Along these blushing borders bright with dew,
And in yon mingled wilderness of flowers,
Fair-handed Spring unbosoms every grace;
Throws out the snow-drop, and the crocus first;
The daisy, primrose, violet darkly blue,
And polyanthus of unnumber'd dyes;
The yellow wall-flower, stained with iron brown;
And lavish stock that scents the garden round:
From the soft wing of vernal breezes shed,
Anemonies; auriculas, enrich'd
With shining meal o'er all their velvet leaves;
And full ranunculas, of glowing red.
Then comes the tulip-race, where Beauty plays
Her idle freaks; from family diffus'd
To family, as flies the father-dust,
The varied colours run; and while they break
On the charm'd eye, the exulting florist marks,
With secret pride, the wonders of his hand.
No gradual bloom is wanting; from the bud,
First-born of Spring, to Summer's musky tribes:
Nor hyacinths, of purest virgin white,
Low bent, and blushing inward; nor jonquils,
Of potent fragrance; nor narcissus fair,
As o'er the fabled fountain hanging still;
Nor broad carnations, nor gray-spotted pinks;
Nor, showered from every bush the damask-rose:
Infinite numbers, delicacies, smells,
With hues on hues expression cannot paint,
The breath of Nature, and her endless bloom.

James Thomson
(1700–1748)

Celandine

Thinking of her had saddened me at first,
Until I saw the sun on the celandines lie
Redoubled, and she stood up like a flame,
A living thing, not what before I nursed,
The shadow I was growing to love almost,
The phantom, not the creature with bright eye
That I had thought never to see, once lost.

She found the celandines of February
Always before us all. Her nature and name
Were like those flowers, and now immediately
For a short swift eternity back she came,
Beautiful, happy simply as when she wore
Her brightest bloom among the winter hues
Of all the world; and I was happy too,
Seeing the blossoms and the maiden who
Had seen them with me Februarys before,
Bending to them as in and out she trod
And laughed, with locks sweeping the mossy sod.

But this was a dream: the flowers were not true,
Until I stooped to pluck from the grass there
One of five petals and I smelt the juice
Which made me sigh, remembering she was no more,
Gone like a never perfectly recalled air.

Edward Thomas
(1878–1917)

Ah Sunflower!

Ah, Sunflower! Weary of time,
Who countest the steps of the Sun;
Seeking after that sweet golden clime,
Where the traveller's journey is done;

Where the Youth pined away with desire,
And the pale Virgin shrouded in snow,
Arise from their graves, and aspire,
Where my sunflower wishes to go.

William Blake
(1757-1827)

Flowers for a Funeral

From *Lycidas*

Ye valleys low where the milde whispers use,
Of shades and wanton winds, and gushing brooks,
On whose fresh lap the swart Star sparely looks,
Throw hither all your quaint enameld eyes,
That on the green terf suck the honied showres,
And purple all the ground with vernal flowres.
Bring the rathe Primrose that forsaken dies.
The tufted Crow-toe, and pale Gessamine,
The white Pink, and the Pansie freakt with jeat,
The glowing Violet.
The Musk-rose, and the well attir'd Woodbine,
With Cowslips wan that hang the pensive head,
And every flower that sad embroidery wears:
Bid Amarantus all his beauty shed,
And Daffadillies fill their cups with tears,
To strew the Laureat Herse where Lycid lies.

John Milton
(1608–1674)

The Year

The crocus, while the days are dark,
　　Unfolds its saffron sheen:
At April's touch, the crudest bark
　　Discovers gems of green.

Then sleep the seasons, full of might;
　　While slowly swells the pod
And rounds the peach, and in the night
　　The mushroom bursts the sod.

The Winter falls; the frozen rut
    Is bound with silver bars;
The snow-drift heaps against the hut;
    And night is pierc'd with stars.

Coventry Patmore
(1823-1896)

The Fair Flower Delice

from: *The Shepherd's Calendar*

Bring hither the Pink and purple Columbine,
  With Gillyflowers:
Bring Coronation and Sops in wine,
  Worn of paramours.
Strow me the ground with Daffadowndillies,
And Cowslips, and Kingcups, and loved Lilies:
  The pretty Pawnce,
  And the Chevisaunce,
Shall match with the fair flower Delice.

Edmund Spenser
(1552–1599)

To the Dandelion

Dear common flower, that grow'st beside the way,
Fringing the dusty road with harmless gold,
First pledge of blithesome May,
Which children pluck, and, full of pride uphold,
High-hearted buccaneers, o'erjoyed that they
An Eldorado in the grass have found.
Which not the rich earth's ample round
May match in wealth, thou art more dear to me
Than all the prouder summer-blooms may be.

Gold such as thine ne'er drew the Spanish prow
Through the primeval hush of Indian seas,
Nor wrinkled the lean brow
Of age, to rob the lover's heart of ease;
'Tis the Spring's largess, which she scatters now
To rich and poor alike, with lavish hand,
Though most hearts never understand
To take it at God's value, but pass by
The offered wealth with unrewarded eye.

James Russell Lowell
(1819-1891)

Daisies

The stars are everywhere tonight,
Above, beneath me and around;
They fill the sky with powdery light
And glimmer from the night-strewn ground;
For where the folded daisies are
In every one I see a star.

And so I know that when I pass
Where no sun's shadow counts the hours
And where the sky was there is grass
And where the stars were there are flowers,
Through the long night in which I lie
Stars will be shining in my sky.

Andrew Young
(1885-1971)

Flower in the Crannied Wall

Flower in the crannied wall,
I pluck you out of the crannies,
I hold you here, root and all, in my hand,
Little flower – but if I could understand
What you are, root and all, and all in all,
I should know what God and man is.

Alfred Lord Tennyson
(1809–1892)

The Lilies of the Field

And why take ye thought for raiment? Consider the lilies of the field, how they grow; they toil not, neither do they spin:

And yet I say unto you, That even Solomon in all his glory Was not arrayed like one of these.

Wherefore, if God so clothe the grass of the field, which to day is, and to morrow is cast into the oven, shall he not much more clothe you, O ye of little faith.

Gospel of St. Matthew vi, 28-30

The Marigold

Mark how the bashful morn in vain
    Courts the amorous Marigold,
With sighing blasts and weeping rain;
    Yet she refuses to unfold.
But when the Planet of the Day
Approacheth with his powerful ray,
    Then she spreads, then she receives
    His warmer beams into her virgin leaves.

Thomas Carew
(1594/5–1640)

Lines Written in Early Spring

I heard a thousand blended notes,
While in a grove I sat reclined,
In that sweet mood when pleasant thoughts
Bring sad thoughts to the mind.

To her fair works did Nature link
The human soul that through me ran;
And much it grieved my heart to think
What man has made of man.

Through primrose tufts, in that green bower,
The periwinkle trailed its wreaths;
And 'tis my faith that every flower
Enjoys the air it breathes.

The birds around me hopped and played,
Their thoughts I cannot measure –
But the least motion which they made,
It seemed a thrill of pleasure.

The budding twigs spread out their fan,
To catch the breezy air;
And I must think, do all I can,
That there was pleasure there.

If this belief from heaven be sent,
If such be Nature's holy plan,
Have I not reason to lament
What man has made of man?

William Wordsworth
(1770–1850)

The Lily

The modest Rose puts forth a thorn,
The humble Sheep a threat'ning horn;
While the Lily white shall in Love delight,
Nor a thorn nor a threat stain her beauty bright.

William Blake
(1757–1827)

Index of Poets

Index for Poems

Picture credits

Batsford archive, pages: 4, 8–9, 55, 77, 81, 85, 87, 91, 96

Art Archive, Amoret Collection,page: 11

Art Archive, CCI, page 29

TFL from the London Transport Museum collection, pages: 15, 19, 21, 23, 27, 31, 35, 37, 40–41, 43, 46, 57, 61, 63, 67, 72–73, 78-79

Acknowledgements

'Whinlands' (from *Door into the Dark*) by Seamus Heaney courtesy of Faber and Faber, London

'The bluebells' by John Masefield courtesy of The Society of Authors as the Literary Representative of the Estate of John Masefield.

'Cowslips' (from *Collected Poems*) by Sachaverell Sitwell reprinted by permission of Peters Fraser & Dunlop (www.petersfraserdunlop.com) on behalf of the Estate of Sachaverell Sitwell.

'The Snowdrop' by Walter de la Mare courtesy of the Literary Trustees of Walter de la Mare and The Society of Authors as their representative

'Daisies' (from *Selected Poems*) by Andrew Young courtesy of Carcanet Press Limited

'The Poppies' by Richard Church reproduced by permission of Pollinger Limited